Goodnight Gratitude Journal

Goodnight Gratitude Journal

Nightly reflections on thankfulness

EMMA VAN HINSBERGH

SIRIUS

All images courtesy of Shutterstock.

SIRIUS

This edition published in 2024 by Sirius Publishing, a division of
Arcturus Publishing Limited,
26/27 Bickels Yard, 151–153 Bermondsey Street,
London SE1 3HA

ISBN: 978-1-3988-4348-6
AD011858NT

Printed in China

INTRODUCTION

Giving thanks for all the good things in your life before you go to bed at night is one of the quickest routes to happiness and wellbeing. Expressing gratitude has been linked to better mental health, decreased anxiety, and improved relationships, and research shows that cultivating a habit of appreciation before you go to bed at night will help you to worry less and get a longer and more restorative sleep. What's more, it can contribute to an optimistic and grateful outlook.

One of the simplest ways to embrace this life-enhancing routine is by keeping a daily journal. Writing your own goodnight gratitude diary to record all the things you have been grateful for during the day has numerous benefits. It encourages mindfulness which has been linked to better mental health, including decreased stress and anxiety and an improved mood.

Expressing gratitude also helps to foster a deeper sense of connection and appreciation for the people in your life and the world around you. Spending a few minutes each evening listing all the people you love and the good things in your life can strengthen your relationships and have a positive knock-on effect on your emotional wellbeing.

By reflecting on positive aspects of your day, you can shift your focus from potential stressors to small, uplifting moments for which you are grateful. This could be anything from the beauty of nature to acts of kindness, from good things that have happened to you to lessons you have learned that day, from your health and wellbeing to the comforts of your surroundings.

Regularly acknowledging these positive aspects of your life can help to create a healthier outlook, even when times are challenging.

It reminds you that there are positive elements in every day, no matter how small and helps you to become more resilient.

What's more, engaging in optimistic and grateful thoughts before bedtime can create a more relaxed mental state, which may contribute to improved sleep quality. So, give thanks for all the blessings in your life and embrace an "attitude of gratitude" before you drift off to the land of nod and you'll wake up on a positive note, feeling ready to embrace everything the day holds.

Some things to remember when you exercise gratitude:

- Establish a gratitude ritual. Set the mood, light a candle, and play gentle music to fully appreciate the moment as you write your journal.
- Try to be specific. This adds authenticity and meaning to your words. For example instead of writing "I am grateful for breakfast with my children", write instead "I am grateful for breakfast with my children because it allowed me share the joy of laughter with them."
- Remember the small things. From the cup of tea you had in the morning to the comfortable slippers you put on in the evening, don't overlook seemingly unimportant moments.
- Acknowledge challenges. Remember that difficult situations can be positive, helping to shift your perspective and build resilience.
- Engage all your senses. Remember how certain sights, sounds and smells contributed to your happiness.
- Big yourself up. Include personal achievements and celebrate even the smallest accomplishments. This helps to build self-worth and esteem.

Evening Gratitude

Today I enjoyed the
daily routine of...

....

because..................................

....

....

....

Today the person I give
thanks and gratitude for is...

....

because ....

....

....

**MEDITATION
ON HAPPINESS**

The most positive
highlight of my day was...

....

....

because ....

....

....

....

My World

One thing that happened
in the world today for which I am
grateful is...

....

this is because..........................

....

....

....

I appreciated nature's powerful energy by...

....
....
....

My small but fulfilling accomplishment today was...

....
....
....

HAPPY THOUGHTS

My positive affirmation of gratitude before I sleep is...

....
....
....

Creative Visualization

Tomorrow I am most looking forward to...

....
....

Evening Gratitude

Today I enjoyed the
daily routine of...

....

because...............................

....

....

....

Today the person I give
thanks and gratitude for is...

....

because ....

....

....

My World
One thing that happened
in the world today for which I am
grateful is...

....

this is because ....

....

....

....

**MEDITATION
ON HAPPINESS**

The most positive
highlight of my day was...

....

....

because ....

....

....

Date ____ / ____ / ____

I appreciated nature's
powerful energy by...

....

....

....

My small but fulfilling
accomplishment today was...

....

....

....

....

HAPPY
THOUGHTS

My positive affirmation of gratitude before I sleep is...

....

....

....

Creative
Visualization

Tomorrow I am most looking forward to...

....

....

Evening Gratitude

Today I enjoyed the
daily routine of...

....

because ....

....

....

Today the person I give
thanks and gratitude for is...

....

because ....

....

....

My World
One thing that happened
in the world today for which I am
grateful is...

....

this is because ....

....

....

**MEDITATION
ON HAPPINESS**

The most positive
highlight of my day was...

....

....

because ....

....

....

....

I appreciated nature's powerful energy by...

....

....

....

My small but fulfilling accomplishment today was...

....

....

....

....

HAPPY THOUGHTS

My positive affirmation of gratitude before I sleep is...

....

....

....

Creative Visualization

Tomorrow I am most looking forward to...

....

....

Evening Gratitude

Today I enjoyed the
daily routine of...

....

because ....

....

....

Today the person I give
thanks and gratitude for is...

....

because ....

....

**MEDITATION
ON HAPPINESS**

The most positive
highlight of my day was...

....

....

because ....

....

....

....

My World
One thing that happened
in the world today for which I am
grateful is...

....

this is because ....

....

....

....

I appreciated nature's powerful energy by...

....

....

....

My small but fulfilling accomplishment today was...

....

....

....

....

HAPPY THOUGHTS

My positive affirmation of gratitude before I sleep is...

....

....

....

Creative Visualization

Tomorrow I am most looking forward to...

....

....

Evening Gratitude

Today I enjoyed the
daily routine of...

....

because...

....

....

....

Today the person I give
thanks and gratitude for is...

....

because ....

....

....

MEDITATION
ON HAPPINESS

The most positive
highlight of my day was...

....

....

because ....

....

....

My World
One thing that happened
in the world today for which I am
grateful is...

....

this is because ....

....

....

....

Date ___ / ___ / ___

I appreciated nature's powerful energy by...

....

....

....

My small but fulfilling accomplishment today was...

....

....

....

....

HAPPY THOUGHTS

My positive affirmation of gratitude before I sleep is...

....

....

....

Creative Visualization

Tomorrow I am most looking forward to...

....

....

Evening Gratitude

Today I enjoyed the
daily routine of...

....

because ....

....

....

....

Today the person I give
thanks and gratitude for is...

....

because ....

....

....

**MEDITATION
ON HAPPINESS**
The most positive
highlight of my day was...

....

....

because ....

....

....

....

My World
One thing that happened
in the world today for which I am
grateful is...

....

this is because ....

....

....

....

Date ___ / ___ / ___

I appreciated nature's
powerful energy by...

....

....

....

....

....

My small but fulfilling
accomplishment today was...

....

....

HAPPY
THOUGHTS

My positive affirmation of gratitude before I sleep is...

....

....

....

Creative
Visualization

Tomorrow I am most looking forward to...

....

....

Evening Gratitude

Today I enjoyed the
daily routine of...

....

because ....

....

....

....

Today the person I give
thanks and gratitude for is...

....

because ....

....

....

My World
One thing that happened
in the world today for which I am
grateful is...

....

this is because ....

....

....

**MEDITATION
ON HAPPINESS**
The most positive
highlight of my day was...

....

....

because

....

....

....

Date ___ / ___ / ___

I appreciated nature's
powerful energy by...

....
....
....

My small but fulfilling
accomplishment today was...

....
....
....
....

HAPPY THOUGHTS

My positive affirmation of gratitude before I sleep is...

....
....
....

Creative Visualization

Tomorrow I am most looking forward to...

....
....

Evening Gratitude

Today I enjoyed the
daily routine of...

....

because....................................

....

....

....

Today the person I give
thanks and gratitude for is...

....

because....................................

....

....

MEDITATION
ON HAPPINESS

The most positive
highlight of my day was...

....

....

because....................................

....

....

....

My World
One thing that happened
in the world today for which I am
grateful is...

....

this is because....................................

....

....

....

Date ___ / ___ / ___

I appreciated nature's powerful energy by...

....

....

....

My small but fulfilling accomplishment today was...

....

....

....

....

HAPPY THOUGHTS

My positive affirmation of gratitude before I sleep is...

....

....

....

Creative Visualization

Tomorrow I am most looking forward to...

....

....

Evening Gratitude

Today I enjoyed the
daily routine of...

....

because ....

....

....

Today the person I give
thanks and gratitude for is...

....

because ....

....

....

MEDITATION ON HAPPINESS

The most positive
highlight of my day was...

....

....

because ....

....

....

My World
One thing that happened
in the world today for which I am
grateful is...

....

this is because ....

....

....

....

Date ___ / ___ / ___

I appreciated nature's
powerful energy by...

....

....

....

My small but fulfilling
accomplishment today was...

....

....

....

....

HAPPY
THOUGHTS

My positive affirmation of gratitude before I sleep is...

....

....

....

Creative
Visualization

Tomorrow I am most looking forward to...

....

....

Evening Gratitude

Today I enjoyed the
daily routine of...

....

because ....

....

....

Today the person I give
thanks and gratitude for is...

....

because ....

....

**MEDITATION
ON HAPPINESS**

The most positive
highlight of my day was...

....

....

because ....

....

....

My World
One thing that happened
in the world today for which I am
grateful is...

....

this is because ....

....

....

Date ___ / ___ / ___

I appreciated nature's
powerful energy by...

....

....

....

My small but fulfilling
accomplishment today was...

....

....

....

....

HAPPY THOUGHTS

My positive affirmation of gratitude before I sleep is...

....

....

....

Creative Visualization

Tomorrow I am most looking forward to...

....

....

Evening Gratitude

Today I enjoyed the
daily routine of...

....

because ....

....

....

....

Today the person I give
thanks and gratitude for is...

....

because ....

....

....

**MEDITATION
ON HAPPINESS**

The most positive
highlight of my day was...

....

....

because ....

....

....

....

My World

One thing that happened
in the world today for which I am
grateful is...

....

this is because ....

....

....

....

I appreciated nature's powerful energy by...

....

....

....

My small but fulfilling accomplishment today was...

....

....

....

....

HAPPY THOUGHTS

My positive affirmation of gratitude before I sleep is...

....

....

....

Creative Visualization

Tomorrow I am most looking forward to...

....

....

Evening Gratitude

Today I enjoyed the
daily routine of...

....

because ....

....

....

....

Today the person I give
thanks and gratitude for is...

....

because ....

....

....

MEDITATION ON HAPPINESS

The most positive
highlight of my day was...

....

....

because ....

....

....

My World
One thing that happened
in the world today for which I am
grateful is...

....

this is because ....

....

....

Date ___ / ___ / ___

I appreciated nature's powerful energy by...

....

....

....

My small but fulfilling accomplishment today was...

....

....

....

....

HAPPY THOUGHTS

My positive affirmation of gratitude before I sleep is...

....

....

....

Creative Visualization

Tomorrow I am most looking forward to...

....

....

Evening Gratitude

Today I enjoyed the
daily routine of...

....

because ....

....

....

Today the person I give
thanks and gratitude for is...

....

because ....

....

....

MEDITATION ON HAPPINESS

The most positive
highlight of my day was...

....

....

because ....

....

....

....

My World

One thing that happened
in the world today for which I am
grateful is...

....

this is because ....

....

....

....

I appreciated nature's powerful energy by...

....

....

....

My small but fulfilling accomplishment today was...

....

....

....

....

HAPPY THOUGHTS

My positive affirmation of gratitude before I sleep is...

....

....

....

Creative Visualization

Tomorrow I am most looking forward to...

....

....

Evening Gratitude

Today I enjoyed the
daily routine of...

....

....

because ....

....

....

....

Today the person I give
thanks and gratitude for is...

....

because ....

....

....

....

My World

One thing that
happened in the world today
for which I am grateful is...

....

....

this is because ....

....

....

....

**MEDITATION
ON HAPPINESS**

The most positive highlight
of my day was...

....

....

because ....

....

....

Date ___ / ___ / ___

I appreciated nature's
powerful energy by...

....

....

....

....

....

....

My small but fulfilling
accomplishment today was...

....

....

....

....

....

....

HAPPY THOUGHTS

My positive affirmation of
gratitude before I sleep is...

....

....

....

....

....

Creative Visualization

Tomorrow I am most looking
forward to...

....

....

....

....

....

Evening Gratitude

Today I enjoyed the
daily routine of...

....

....

because ....

....

....

....

Today the person I give
thanks and gratitude for is...

....

because ....

....

....

....

My World

One thing that
happened in the world today
for which I am grateful is...

....

....

this is because ....

....

....

MEDITATION
ON HAPPINESS

The most positive highlight
of my day was...

....

....

because ....

....

....

Date ___ / ___ / ___

I appreciated nature's
powerful energy by...

....
....
....
....
....
....

My small but fulfilling
accomplishment today was...

....
....
....
....
....
....

HAPPY THOUGHTS

My positive affirmation of
gratitude before I sleep is...

....
....
....
....
....

Creative Visualization

Tomorrow I am most looking
forward to...

....
....
....
....
....

Evening Gratitude

Today I enjoyed the
daily routine of...

....

....

because ....

....

....

....

Today the person I give
thanks and gratitude for is...

....

because ....

....

....

....

My World

One thing that
happened in the world today
for which I am grateful is...

....

....

this is because ....

....

....

....

MEDITATION
ON HAPPINESS

The most positive highlight
of my day was...

....

....

because ....

....

....

Date ___ / ___ / ___

I appreciated nature's
powerful energy by...

....

....

....

....

....

....

My small but fulfilling
accomplishment today was...

....

....

....

....

....

....

HAPPY THOUGHTS

My positive affirmation of
gratitude before I sleep is...

....

....

....

....

....

Creative Visualization

Tomorrow I am most looking
forward to...

....

....

....

....

....

Evening Gratitude

Today I enjoyed the
daily routine of...

....

....

because ....

....

....

....

....

Today the person I give
thanks and gratitude for is...

....

because ....

....

....

....

My World

One thing that
happened in the world today
for which I am grateful is...

....

....

this is because ....

....

....

....

MEDITATION
ON HAPPINESS

The most positive highlight
of my day was...

....

....

because ....

....

....

Date ___ / ___ / ___

I appreciated nature's
powerful energy by...

....

....

....

....

....

....

My small but fulfilling
accomplishment today was...

....

....

....

....

....

....

HAPPY THOUGHTS

My positive affirmation of
gratitude before I sleep is...

....

....

....

....

....

Creative Visualization

Tomorrow I am most looking
forward to...

....

....

....

....

....

Evening Gratitude

Today I enjoyed the
daily routine of...

....

....

because ....

....

....

....

Today the person I give
thanks and gratitude for is...

....

because ....

....

....

....

My World

One thing that
happened in the world today
for which I am grateful is...

....

....

this is because ....

....

....

MEDITATION
ON HAPPINESS

The most positive highlight
of my day was...

....

....

because ....

....

....

Date ___ / ___ / ___

I appreciated nature's
powerful energy by...

....

....

....

....

....

....

My small but fulfilling
accomplishment today was...

....

....

....

....

....

....

HAPPY THOUGHTS

My positive affirmation of
gratitude before I sleep is...

....

....

....

....

....

Creative Visualization

Tomorrow I am most looking
forward to...

....

....

....

....

....

Evening Gratitude

Today I enjoyed the
daily routine of...

....

....

because ....

....

....

Today the person I give
thanks and gratitude for is...

....

because ....

....

....

My World
One thing that
happened in the world today
for which I am grateful is...

....

....

this is because ....

....

....

MEDITATION ON HAPPINESS
The most positive highlight
of my day was...

....

....

because ....

....

....

Date ___ / ___ / ___

I appreciated nature's
powerful energy by...

....

....

....

....

....

....

My small but fulfilling
accomplishment today was...

....

....

....

....

....

....

HAPPY THOUGHTS

My positive affirmation of
gratitude before I sleep is...

....

....

....

....

....

Creative Visualization

Tomorrow I am most looking
forward to...

....

....

....

....

....

Evening Gratitude

Today I enjoyed the
daily routine of...

....

....

because ....

....

....

....

....

Today the person I give
thanks and gratitude for is...

....

because ....

....

....

....

....

My World

One thing that
happened in the world today
for which I am grateful is...

....

....

this is because ....

....

....

....

MEDITATION
ON HAPPINESS

The most positive highlight
of my day was...

....

....

because ....

....

....

....

Date ____ / ____ / ____

I appreciated nature's
powerful energy by...

....

....

....

....

....

....

My small but fulfilling
accomplishment today was...

....

....

....

....

....

....

HAPPY THOUGHTS

My positive affirmation of
gratitude before I sleep is...

....

....

....

....

....

....

Creative Visualization

Tomorrow I am most looking
forward to...

....

....

....

....

....

....

Evening Gratitude

Today I enjoyed the
daily routine of...

....

....

because ....

....

....

....

Today the person I give
thanks and gratitude for is...

....

because ....

....

....

....

My World

One thing that
happened in the world today
for which I am grateful is...

....

....

this is because ....

....

....

....

**MEDITATION
ON HAPPINESS**

The most positive highlight
of my day was...

....

....

because ....

....

....

....

Date ___ / ___ / ___

I appreciated nature's
powerful energy by...

....

....

....

....

....

....

My small but fulfilling
accomplishment today was...

....

....

....

....

....

....

HAPPY THOUGHTS

My positive affirmation of
gratitude before I sleep is...

....

....

....

....

....

Creative Visualization

Tomorrow I am most looking
forward to...

....

....

....

....

....

Evening Gratitude

Today I enjoyed the
daily routine of...

....

....

because ....

....

....

....

Today the person I give
thanks and gratitude for is...

....

because ....

....

....

....

My World

One thing that
happened in the world today
for which I am grateful is...

....

....

this is because ....

....

....

MEDITATION
ON HAPPINESS

The most positive highlight
of my day was...

....

....

because ....

....

....

Date ___ / ___ / ___

I appreciated nature's
powerful energy by...

....

....

....

....

....

....

....

My small but fulfilling
accomplishment today was...

....

....

....

....

....

....

....

HAPPY THOUGHTS

My positive affirmation of
gratitude before I sleep is...

....

....

....

....

....

Creative Visualization

Tomorrow I am most looking
forward to...

....

....

....

....

....

51

Evening Gratitude

Today I enjoyed the
daily routine of...

....
....

because ....
....
....
....

Today the person I give
thanks and gratitude for is...

....

because ....
....
....
....

My World

One thing that
happened in the world today
for which I am grateful is...

....
....

this is because ....
....
....

MEDITATION
ON HAPPINESS

The most positive highlight
of my day was...

....
....

because ....
....
....

Date ___ / ___ / ___

I appreciated nature's
powerful energy by...

....

....

....

....

....

....

My small but fulfilling
accomplishment today was...

....

....

....

....

....

....

HAPPY THOUGHTS

My positive affirmation of
gratitude before I sleep is...

....

....

....

....

....

Creative Visualization

Tomorrow I am most looking
forward to...

....

....

....

....

....

Evening Gratitude

Today I enjoyed the
daily routine of...

....

....

because ....

....

....

....

Today the person I give
thanks and gratitude for is...

....

because ....

....

....

....

My World

One thing that
happened in the world today
for which I am grateful is...

....

....

this is because ....

....

....

MEDITATION
ON HAPPINESS

The most positive highlight
of my day was...

....

....

because ....

....

....

I appreciated nature's
powerful energy by...

My small but fulfilling
accomplishment today was...

....

....

....

....

....

....

HAPPY THOUGHTS

My positive affirmation of
gratitude before I sleep is...

Creative Visualization

Tomorrow I am most looking
forward to...

....

....

....

....

....

Evening Gratitude

Today I enjoyed the
daily routine of...

....

....

because ....

....

....

....

....

Today the person I give
thanks and gratitude for is...

....

because ....

....

....

....

My World

One thing that
happened in the world today
for which I am grateful is...

....

....

this is because ....

....

....

....

**MEDITATION
ON HAPPINESS**

The most positive highlight
of my day was...

....

....

because ....

....

....

Date ___ / ___ / ___

I appreciated nature's
powerful energy by...

....

....

....

....

....

....

My small but fulfilling
accomplishment today was...

....

....

....

....

....

....

HAPPY THOUGHTS

My positive affirmation of
gratitude before I sleep is...

....

....

....

....

....

Creative Visualization

Tomorrow I am most looking
forward to...

....

....

....

....

Evening Gratitude

Today I enjoyed the
daily routine of...

....

....

because ....

....

....

Today the person I give
thanks and gratitude for is...

....

because ....

....

....

....

My World

One thing that
happened in the world today
for which I am grateful is...

....

....

this is because ....

....

....

MEDITATION
ON HAPPINESS

The most positive highlight
of my day was...

....

....

because ....

....

....

Date ___ / ___ / ___

I appreciated nature's
powerful energy by...

My small but fulfilling
accomplishment today was...

....

....

....

....

....

....

....

....

....

....

....

....

....

....

HAPPY THOUGHTS

My positive affirmation of
gratitude before I sleep is...

Creative Visualization

Tomorrow I am most looking
forward to...

....

....

....

....

....

....

....

....

....

....

Evening Gratitude

Today I enjoyed the daily routine of...

....

because ....

....

Today the person I give thanks and gratitude for is...

....

because ....

....

My World

One thing that happened in the
world today for which I am grateful is...

....

this is because ....

....

MEDITATION ON HAPPINESS

The most positive highlight of my day was...

....

because ....

....

I appreciated nature's powerful energy by...

....

....

....

My small but fulfilling accomplishment today was...

....

....

....

HAPPY THOUGHTS

My positive affirmation of gratitude before I sleep is...

....

....

Creative Visualization

Tomorrow I am most looking forward to...

....

....

Evening Gratitude

Today I enjoyed the daily routine of...

....

because ....

....

Today the person I give thanks and gratitude for is...

....

because ....

....

My World

One thing that happened in the
world today for which I am grateful is...

....

this is because ....

....

MEDITATION ON HAPPINESS

The most positive highlight of my day was...

....

because ....

....

Date ___ / ___ / ___

I appreciated nature's powerful energy by...

....

....

....

My small but fulfilling accomplishment today was...

....

....

....

HAPPY THOUGHTS

My positive affirmation of gratitude before I sleep is...

....

....

Creative Visualization

Tomorrow I am most looking forward to...

....

....

Evening Gratitude

Today I enjoyed the daily routine of...

....

because ....

....

Today the person I give thanks and gratitude for is...

....

because ....

....

My World
One thing that happened in the
world today for which I am grateful is...

....

this is because ....

....

MEDITATION ON HAPPINESS
The most positive highlight of my day was...

....

because ....

....

Date ____ / ____ / ____

I appreciated nature's powerful energy by...

....

....

....

My small but fulfilling accomplishment today was...

....

....

....

HAPPY THOUGHTS

My positive affirmation of gratitude before I sleep is...

....

....

Creative Visualization

Tomorrow I am most looking forward to...

....

....

Evening Gratitude

Today I enjoyed the daily routine of...

....

because ....

....

Today the person I give thanks and gratitude for is...

....

because ....

....

My World
One thing that happened in the
world today for which I am grateful is...

....

this is because ....

....

MEDITATION ON HAPPINESS
The most positive highlight of my day was...

....

because ....

....

Date ___ / ___ / ___

I appreciated nature's powerful energy by...

....

....

....

My small but fulfilling accomplishment today was...

....

....

....

HAPPY THOUGHTS

My positive affirmation of gratitude before I sleep is...

....

....

Creative Visualization

Tomorrow I am most looking forward to...

....

....

Evening Gratitude

Today I enjoyed the daily routine of...

....

because ....

....

Today the person I give thanks and gratitude for is...

....

because ....

....

My World

One thing that happened in the
world today for which I am grateful is...

....

this is because ....

....

MEDITATION ON HAPPINESS

The most positive highlight of my day was...

....

because ....

....

Date ___ / ___ / ___

I appreciated nature's powerful energy by...

....

....

....

My small but fulfilling accomplishment today was...

....

....

....

HAPPY THOUGHTS

My positive affirmation of gratitude before I sleep is...

....

....

Creative Visualization

Tomorrow I am most looking forward to...

....

....

Evening Gratitude

Today I enjoyed the daily routine of...

....

because ....

....

Today the person I give thanks and gratitude for is...

....

because ....

....

My World
One thing that happened in the
world today for which I am grateful is...

....

this is because ....

....

MEDITATION ON HAPPINESS
The most positive highlight of my day was...

....

because ....

....

Date ___ / ___ / ___

I appreciated nature's powerful energy by...

....

....

....

My small but fulfilling accomplishment today was...

....

....

....

HAPPY THOUGHTS

My positive affirmation of gratitude before I sleep is...

....

....

Creative Visualization

Tomorrow I am most looking forward to...

....

....

Evening Gratitude

Today I enjoyed the daily routine of...

....

because ....

....

Today the person I give thanks and gratitude for is...

....

because ....

....

My World

One thing that happened in the
world today for which I am grateful is...

....

this is because ....

....

MEDITATION ON HAPPINESS

The most positive highlight of my day was...

....

because ....

....

I appreciated nature's powerful energy by...

....

....

....

My small but fulfilling accomplishment today was...

....

....

....

HAPPY THOUGHTS

My positive affirmation of gratitude before I sleep is...

....

....

Creative Visualization

Tomorrow I am most looking forward to...

....

....

Evening Gratitude

Today I enjoyed the daily routine of...

....

because ....

....

Today the person I give thanks and gratitude for is...

....

because ....

....

My World

One thing that happened in the
world today for which I am grateful is...

....

this is because ....

....

MEDITATION ON HAPPINESS

The most positive highlight of my day was...

....

because ....

....

Date ___ / ___ / ___

I appreciated nature's powerful energy by...

....

....

....

My small but fulfilling accomplishment today was...

....

....

....

HAPPY THOUGHTS

My positive affirmation of gratitude before I sleep is...

....

....

Creative Visualization

Tomorrow I am most looking forward to...

....

....

Evening Gratitude

Today I enjoyed the daily routine of...

....

because ....

....

Today the person I give thanks and gratitude for is...

....

because ....

....

My World

One thing that happened in the
world today for which I am grateful is...

....

this is because ....

....

MEDITATION ON HAPPINESS

The most positive highlight of my day was...

....

because ....

....

Date ___ / ___ / ___

I appreciated nature's powerful energy by...

....

....

....

My small but fulfilling accomplishment today was...

....

....

....

HAPPY THOUGHTS

My positive affirmation of gratitude before I sleep is...

....

....

Creative Visualization

Tomorrow I am most looking forward to...

....

....

Evening Gratitude

Today I enjoyed the daily routine of...

....

because ....

....

Today the person I give thanks and gratitude for is...

....

because ....

....

My World

One thing that happened in the
world today for which I am grateful is...

....

this is because ....

....

MEDITATION ON HAPPINESS

The most positive highlight of my day was...

....

because ....

....

Date ___ / ___ / ___

I appreciated nature's powerful energy by...

....

....

....

My small but fulfilling accomplishment today was...

....

....

....

HAPPY THOUGHTS

My positive affirmation of gratitude before I sleep is...

....

....

Creative Visualization

Tomorrow I am most looking forward to...

....

....

Evening Gratitude

Today I enjoyed the daily routine of...

....

because ....

....

Today the person I give thanks and gratitude for is...

....

because ....

....

My World

One thing that happened in the
world today for which I am grateful is...

....

this is because ....

....

MEDITATION ON HAPPINESS

The most positive highlight of my day was...

....

because ....

....

Date ___ / ___ / ___

I appreciated nature's powerful energy by...

....

....

....

My small but fulfilling accomplishment today was...

....

....

....

HAPPY THOUGHTS

My positive affirmation of gratitude before I sleep is...

....

....

Creative Visualization

Tomorrow I am most looking forward to...

....

....

Evening Gratitude

Today I enjoyed the daily routine of...

....

because ....

....

Today the person I give thanks and gratitude for is...

....

because ....

....

My World

One thing that happened in the
world today for which I am grateful is...

....

this is because ....

....

MEDITATION ON HAPPINESS

The most positive highlight of my day was...

....

because ....

....

I appreciated nature's powerful energy by...

....

....

....

My small but fulfilling accomplishment today was...

....

....

....

HAPPY THOUGHTS
My positive affirmation of gratitude before I sleep is...

....

....

Creative Visualization
Tomorrow I am most looking forward to...

....

....

Evening Gratitude

Today I enjoyed the daily routine of...

....

because ....

....

Today the person I give thanks and gratitude for is...

....

because ....

....

My World

One thing that happened in the
world today for which I am grateful is...

....

this is because ....

....

MEDITATION ON HAPPINESS

The most positive highlight of my day was...

....

because ....

....

Date ____ / ____ / ____

I appreciated nature's powerful energy by...

....

....

....

My small but fulfilling accomplishment today was...

....

....

....

HAPPY THOUGHTS

My positive affirmation of gratitude before I sleep is...

....

....

Creative Visualization

Tomorrow I am most looking forward to...

....

....

Evening Gratitude

Today I enjoyed the daily routine of...

....

....

because ....

....

....

Today
the person
I give thanks and gratitude for is...

....

because ....

....

....

My World

One thing that happened
in the world today for which
I am grateful is...

....

this is because ....

....

MEDITATION ON HAPPINESS

The most positive highlight of my day was...

....

because ....

Date ___ / ___ / ___

I appreciated nature's powerful energy by...

....

....

My small but fulfilling accomplishment today was...

....

....

HAPPY THOUGHTS

My positive affirmation of gratitude before I sleep is...

....

....

....

Creative Visualization

Tomorrow I am most looking forward to...

....

Evening Gratitude

Today I enjoyed the daily routine of...

....

....

because ....

....

....

Today
the person
I give thanks and gratitude for is...

....

because ....

....

....

My World

One thing that happened
in the world today for which
I am grateful is...

....

this is because ....

....

MEDITATION ON HAPPINESS

The most positive highlight of my day was...

....

because ....

Date ___ / ___ / ___

I appreciated nature's powerful energy by...

....

....

My small but fulfilling accomplishment today was...

....

....

HAPPY THOUGHTS

My positive affirmation of gratitude before I sleep is...

....

....

....

Creative Visualization

Tomorrow I am most looking forward to...

....

Evening Gratitude

Today I enjoyed the daily routine of...

....

....

because ....

....

....

My World
One thing that happened
in the world today for which
I am grateful is...

....

this is because ....

....

Today
the person
I give thanks and gratitude for is...

....

because ....

....

....

MEDITATION ON HAPPINESS
The most positive highlight of my day was...

....

because ....

I appreciated nature's powerful energy by...

....

....

My small but fulfilling accomplishment today was...

....

....

HAPPY
THOUGHTS

My positive affirmation of gratitude before I sleep is...

....

....

....

Creative Visualization

Tomorrow I am most looking forward to...

....

Evening Gratitude

Today I enjoyed the daily routine of...

....

....

because ....

....

....

Today
the person
I give thanks and gratitude for is...

....

because ....

....

....

My World

One thing that happened
in the world today for which
I am grateful is...

....

this is because ....

....

MEDITATION ON HAPPINESS

The most positive highlight of my day was...

....

because ....

Date ___ / ___ / ___

I appreciated nature's powerful energy by...

....

....

My small but fulfilling accomplishment today was...

....

....

HAPPY THOUGHTS

My positive affirmation of gratitude before I sleep is...

....

....

....

Creative Visualization

Tomorrow I am most looking forward to...

....

Evening Gratitude

Today I enjoyed the daily routine of...

....

....

because ....

....

....

Today
the person
I give thanks and gratitude for is...

....

because ....

....

....

My World

One thing that happened
in the world today for which
I am grateful is...

....

this is because ....

....

MEDITATION ON HAPPINESS

The most positive highlight of my day was...

....

because ....

I appreciated nature's powerful energy by...

....

....

My small but fulfilling accomplishment today was...

....

....

HAPPY THOUGHTS

My positive affirmation of gratitude before I sleep is...

....

....

....

Creative Visualization

Tomorrow I am most looking forward to...

....

Evening Gratitude

Today I enjoyed the daily routine of...

....

....

because ....

....

....

Today
the person
I give thanks and gratitude for is...

....

because ....

....

....

My World

One thing that happened
in the world today for which
I am grateful is...

....

this is because ....

....

MEDITATION ON HAPPINESS

The most positive highlight of my day was...

....

because ....

I appreciated nature's powerful energy by...

....

....

My small but fulfilling accomplishment today was...

....

....

HAPPY
THOUGHTS

My positive affirmation of gratitude before I sleep is...

....

....

....

Creative Visualization

Tomorrow I am most looking forward to...

....

Evening Gratitude

Today I enjoyed the daily routine of...

....

....

because ....

....

....

the ...... on
I give thanks and gratitude for is...

....

because ....

....

....

My World

One thing that happened
in the world today for which
I am grateful is...

....

this is because ....

....

MEDITATION ON HAPPINESS

The most positive highlight of my day was...

....

because ....

I appreciated nature's powerful energy by...

....

....

My small but fulfilling accomplishment today was...

....

....

HAPPY THOUGHTS

My positive affirmation of gratitude before I sleep is...

....

....

....

Creative Visualization

Tomorrow I am most looking forward to...

....

Evening Gratitude

Today I enjoyed the daily routine of...

....

....

because ....

....

....

Today
the person
I give thanks and gratitude for is...

....

because ....

....

....

My World

One thing that happened
in the world today for which
I am grateful is...

....

this is because ....

....

MEDITATION ON HAPPINESS

The most positive highlight of my day was...

....

because ....

I appreciated nature's powerful energy by...

....

....

My small but fulfilling accomplishment today was...

....

....

HAPPY THOUGHTS

My positive affirmation of gratitude before I sleep is...

....

....

....

Creative Visualization

Tomorrow I am most looking forward to...

....

Evening Gratitude

Today I enjoyed the daily routine of...

....

....

because ....

....

....

Today
the person
I give thanks and gratitude for is...

....

because ....

....

....

My World

One thing that happened
in the world today for which
I am grateful is...

....

this is because ....

....

MEDITATION ON HAPPINESS

The most positive highlight of my day was...

....

because ....

I appreciated nature's powerful energy by...

....

....

My small but fulfilling accomplishment today was...

....

....

HAPPY THOUGHTS

My positive affirmation of gratitude before I sleep is...

....

....

....

Creative Visualization

Tomorrow I am most looking forward to...

....

Evening Gratitude

Today I enjoyed the daily routine of...

....

....

because ....

....

....

Today
the person
I give thanks and gratitude for is...

....

because ....

....

....

My World

One thing that happened
in the world today for which
I am grateful is...

....

this is because ....

....

MEDITATION ON HAPPINESS

The most positive highlight of my day was...

....

because ....

Date ___ / ___ / ___

I appreciated nature's powerful energy by...

....

....

My small but fulfilling accomplishment today was...

....

....

HAPPY THOUGHTS

My positive affirmation of gratitude before I sleep is...

....

....

....

Creative Visualization

Tomorrow I am most looking forward to...

....

Evening Gratitude

Today I enjoyed the daily routine of...

....

....

because ....

....

....

Today
the person
I give thanks and gratitude for is...

....

because ....

....

....

My World
One thing that happened
in the world today for which
I am grateful is...

....

this is because ....

....

MEDITATION ON HAPPINESS
The most positive highlight of my day was...

....

because ....

I appreciated nature's powerful energy by...

....

....

My small but fulfilling accomplishment today was...

....

....

HAPPY THOUGHTS

My positive affirmation of gratitude before I sleep is...

....

....

....

Creative Visualization

Tomorrow I am most looking forward to...

....

Evening Gratitude

Today I enjoyed the daily routine of...

....

....

because ....

....

....

Today
the person
I give thanks and gratitude for is...

....

because ....

....

....

My World

One thing that happened
in the world today for which
I am grateful is...

....

this is because ....

....

MEDITATION ON HAPPINESS

The most positive highlight of my day was...

....

because ....

I appreciated nature's powerful energy by...

....

....

My small but fulfilling accomplishment today was...

....

....

HAPPY THOUGHTS

My positive affirmation of gratitude before I sleep is...

....

....

....

Creative Visualization

Tomorrow I am most looking forward to...

....

Evening Gratitude

Today I enjoyed the daily routine of...

....

....

because ....

....

....

My World

One thing that happened
in the world today for which
I am grateful is...

Today
the person
I give thanks and gratitude for is...

....

because ....

....

....

....

this is because ....

....

MEDITATION ON HAPPINESS

The most positive highlight of my day was...

....

because ....

I appreciated nature's powerful energy by...

....

....

My small but fulfilling accomplishment today was...

....

....

HAPPY THOUGHTS

My positive affirmation of gratitude before I sleep is...

....

....

....

Creative Visualization

Tomorrow I am most looking forward to...

....

Evening Gratitude

Today I enjoyed the daily routine of...

....

because ....

• • •

Today the person I give thanks and gratitude for is...

....

because ....

• • • •

My World

One thing that happened in the world today for which I am grateful is...

....

this is because ....

• • • • •

MEDITATION ON HAPPINESS

The most positive highlight of my day was...

....

because ....

Date ___ / ___ / ___

I appreciated nature's powerful energy by...

....

....

My small but fulfilling accomplishment today was...

....

....

....

HAPPY THOUGHTS

My positive affirmation of gratitude before I sleep is...

....

....

....

Creative Visualization

Tomorrow I am most looking forward to...

....

....

....

Evening Gratitude

Today I enjoyed the daily routine of...

....

because ....

• • •

Today the person I give thanks and gratitude for is...

....

because ....

• • • •

My World

One thing that happened in the world today for which I am grateful is...

....

this is because ....

• • • • •

MEDITATION ON HAPPINESS

The most positive highlight of my day was...

....

because ....

I appreciated nature's powerful energy by...

....

....

My small but fulfilling accomplishment today was...

....

....

....

HAPPY THOUGHTS

My positive affirmation of gratitude before I sleep is...

....

....

....

Creative Visualization

Tomorrow I am most looking forward to...

....

....

....

Evening Gratitude

Today I enjoyed the daily routine of...

....

because ....

—————————— • • • ——————————

Today the person I give thanks and gratitude for is...

....

because ....

—————————— • • • • ——————————

My World

One thing that happened in the world today for which I am grateful is...

....

this is because ....

—————————— • • • • • ——————————

MEDITATION ON HAPPINESS

The most positive highlight of my day was...

....

because ....

I appreciated nature's powerful energy by...

....

....

My small but fulfilling accomplishment today was...

....

....

....

HAPPY THOUGHTS

My positive affirmation of gratitude before I sleep is...

....

....

....

Creative Visualization

Tomorrow I am most looking forward to...

....

....

....

Evening Gratitude

Today I enjoyed the daily routine of...

....

because ....

· · ·

Today the person I give thanks and gratitude for is...

....

because ....

· · · ·

My World

One thing that happened in the world today for which I am grateful is...

....

this is because ....

· · · · ·

MEDITATION ON HAPPINESS

The most positive highlight of my day was...

....

because ....

I appreciated nature's powerful energy by...

....

....

My small but fulfilling accomplishment today was...

....

....

....

HAPPY THOUGHTS

My positive affirmation of gratitude before I sleep is...

....

....

....

Creative Visualization

Tomorrow I am most looking forward to...

....

....

....

Evening Gratitude

Today I enjoyed the daily routine of...

....

because ....

— — — • • • — —

Today the person I give thanks and gratitude for is...

....

because ....

— — — • • • • — —

My World

One thing that happened in the world today for which I am grateful is...

....

this is because ....

— — — • • • • • — —

MEDITATION ON HAPPINESS

The most positive highlight of my day was...

....

because ....

Date ___ / ___ / ___

I appreciated nature's powerful energy by...

....

....

My small but fulfilling accomplishment today was...

....

....

....

HAPPY THOUGHTS

My positive affirmation of gratitude before I sleep is...

....

....

....

Creative Visualization

Tomorrow I am most looking forward to...

....

....

....

Evening Gratitude

Today I enjoyed the daily routine of...

....

because ....

— — — — — • • • — — —

Today the person I give thanks and gratitude for is...

....

because ....

— — — — — • • • • — — —

My World
One thing that happened in the world today for which I am grateful is...

....

this is because ....

— — — — • • • • • — — —

MEDITATION ON HAPPINESS
The most positive highlight of my day was...

....

because ....

I appreciated nature's powerful energy by...

....

....

My small but fulfilling accomplishment today was...

....

....

....

HAPPY THOUGHTS

My positive affirmation of gratitude before I sleep is...

....

....

....

Creative Visualization

Tomorrow I am most looking forward to...

....

....

....

Evening Gratitude

Today I enjoyed the daily routine of...

....

because ....

— • • • —

Today the person I give thanks and gratitude for is...

....

because ....

— • • • • —

My World

One thing that happened in the world today for which I am grateful is...

....

this is because ....

MEDITATION ON HAPPINESS

The most positive highlight of my day was...

....

because ....

Date ___ / ___ / ___

I appreciated nature's powerful energy by...

....

....

My small but fulfilling accomplishment today was...

....

....

....

HAPPY THOUGHTS

My positive affirmation of gratitude before I sleep is...

....

....

....

Creative Visualization

Tomorrow I am most looking forward to...

....

....

....

Evening Gratitude

Today I enjoyed the daily routine of...

....

because ....

• • •

Today the person I give thanks and gratitude for is...

....

because ....

• • • •

My World

One thing that happened in the world today for which I am grateful is...

....

this is because ....

• • • • •

MEDITATION ON HAPPINESS

The most positive highlight of my day was...

....

because ....

I appreciated nature's powerful energy by...

....

....

My small but fulfilling accomplishment today was...

....

....

....

HAPPY THOUGHTS

My positive affirmation of gratitude before I sleep is...

....

....

....

Creative Visualization

Tomorrow I am most looking forward to...

....

....

....

Evening Gratitude

Today I enjoyed the daily routine of...

....

because ....

—————————————— • • • ——————————

Today the person I give thanks and gratitude for is...

....

because ....

—————————————— • • • • ——————————

My World

One thing that happened in the world today for which I am grateful is...

....

this is because ....

—————————— • • • • • ——————————

MEDITATION ON HAPPINESS

The most positive highlight of my day was...

....

because ....

I appreciated nature's powerful energy by...

....

....

My small but fulfilling accomplishment today was...

....

....

....

HAPPY THOUGHTS

My positive affirmation of gratitude before I sleep is...

....

....

....

Creative Visualization

Tomorrow I am most looking forward to...

....

....

....

Evening Gratitude

Today I enjoyed the daily routine of...

....

because ....

———————————— • • • ————————————

Today the person I give thanks and gratitude for is...

....

because ....

———————————— • • • • ————————————

My World

One thing that happened in the world today for which I am grateful is...

....

this is because ....

• • • • •

MEDITATION ON HAPPINESS

The most positive highlight of my day was...

....

because ....

I appreciated nature's powerful energy by...

....

....

My small but fulfilling accomplishment today was...

....

....

....

HAPPY THOUGHTS

My positive affirmation of gratitude before I sleep is...

....

....

....

Creative Visualization

Tomorrow I am most looking forward to...

....

....

....

Evening Gratitude

Today I enjoyed the daily routine of...

....

because ....

— — — • • • — —

Today the person I give thanks and gratitude for is...

....

because ....

— — — • • • • — —

My World

One thing that happened in the world today for which I am grateful is...

....

this is because ....

— — — • • • • • — —

MEDITATION ON HAPPINESS

The most positive highlight of my day was...

....

because ....

I appreciated nature's powerful energy by...

....

....

My small but fulfilling accomplishment today was...

....

....

....

HAPPY THOUGHTS

My positive affirmation of gratitude before I sleep is...

....

....

....

Creative Visualization

Tomorrow I am most looking forward to...

....

....

....

Evening Gratitude

Today I enjoyed the daily routine of...

....

because ....

• • •

Today the person I give thanks and gratitude for is...

....

because ....

• • • •

My World

One thing that happened in the world today for which I am grateful is...

....

this is because ....

• • • • •

MEDITATION ON HAPPINESS

The most positive highlight of my day was...

....

because ....

Date ___ / ___ / ___

I appreciated nature's powerful energy by...

....

....

My small but fulfilling accomplishment today was...

....

....

....

HAPPY THOUGHTS

My positive affirmation of gratitude before I sleep is...

....

....

....

Creative Visualization

Tomorrow I am most looking forward to...

....

....

....

Evening Gratitude

Today I enjoyed the daily routine of...

....

because ....

• • •

Today the person I give thanks and gratitude for is...

....

because ....

• • • •

My World
One thing that happened in the world today for which I am grateful is...

....

this is because ....

• • • • •

MEDITATION ON HAPPINESS
The most positive highlight of my day was...

....

because ....

I appreciated nature's powerful energy by...

....

....

My small but fulfilling accomplishment today was...

....

....

....

HAPPY THOUGHTS

My positive affirmation of gratitude before I sleep is...

....

....

....

Creative Visualization

Tomorrow I am most looking forward to...

....

....

....

Evening Gratitude

Today I enjoyed
the daily routine of...

....

....

because ....

....

....

....

....

Today the person I give
thanks and gratitude for is...

....

....

because ....

....

....

....

....

My World

One thing that happened
in the world today for which
I am grateful is...

....

....

this is because ....

....

....

....

MEDITATION ON HAPPINESS

The most positive highlight
of my day was...

....

....

because ....

....

....

....

I appreciated nature's powerful energy by...

....

....

....

....

HAPPY THOUGHTS

My positive affirmation of gratitude before I sleep is...

....

....

....

....

....

....

My small but fulfilling accomplishment today was...

....

....

....

....

....

Creative Visualization

Tomorrow I am most looking forward to...

....

....

....

....

....

....

Evening Gratitude

Today I enjoyed the daily routine of...

....
....
because ....
....
....
....

Today the person I give thanks and gratitude for is...

....
....
because ....
....
....
....

My World

One thing that happened
in the world today for which
I am grateful is...

....
....
this is because ....
....
....
....

MEDITATION ON HAPPINESS

The most positive highlight
of my day was...

....
....
because ....
....
....
....

I appreciated nature's
powerful energy by...

....

....

....

....

HAPPY THOUGHTS

My positive affirmation of
gratitude before I sleep is...

....

....

....

....

....

....

My
small but
fulfilling accomplishment
today was...

....

....

....

....

....

Creative Visualization

Tomorrow I am most
looking forward to...

....

....

....

....

....

....

Evening Gratitude

Today I enjoyed the daily routine of...

....

....

because ....

....

....

....

Today the person I give thanks and gratitude for is...

....

....

because ....

....

....

....

My World

One thing that happened
in the world today for which
I am grateful is...

....

....

this is because ....

....

....

MEDITATION ON HAPPINESS

The most positive highlight
of my day was...

....

....

because ....

....

....

I appreciated nature's
powerful energy by...

....

....

....

....

HAPPY THOUGHTS

My positive affirmation of
gratitude before I sleep is...

....

....

....

....

....

....

My
small but
fulfilling accomplishment
today was...

....

....

....

....

....

Creative Visualization

Tomorrow I am most
looking forward to...

....

....

....

....

....

....

Evening Gratitude

Today I enjoyed
the daily routine of...

....

....

because ....

....

....

....

....

Today the person I give
thanks and gratitude for is...

....

....

because ....

....

....

....

....

My World

One thing that happened
in the world today for which
I am grateful is...

....

....

this is because ....

....

....

....

MEDITATION ON HAPPINESS

The most positive highlight
of my day was...

....

....

because ....

....

....

I appreciated nature's
powerful energy by...

....

....

....

....

HAPPY THOUGHTS
My positive affirmation of
gratitude before I sleep is...

....

....

....

....

....

....

My
small but
fulfilling accomplishment
today was...

....

....

....

....

Creative Visualization
Tomorrow I am most
looking forward to...

....

....

....

....

....

Evening Gratitude

Today I enjoyed
the daily routine of...

....

....

because ....

....

....

....

Today the person I give
thanks and gratitude for is...

....

....

because ....

....

....

....

My World

One thing that happened
in the world today for which
I am grateful is...

....

....

this is because ....

....

....

....

MEDITATION ON HAPPINESS

The most positive highlight
of my day was...

....

....

because ....

....

....

I appreciated nature's
powerful energy by...

....

....

....

....

HAPPY THOUGHTS

My positive affirmation of

gratitude before I sleep is...

....

....

....

....

....

....

My
small but
fulfilling accomplishment
today was...

....

....

....

....

....

Creative Visualization

Tomorrow I am most

looking forward to...

....

....

....

....

....

....

Evening Gratitude

Today I enjoyed
the daily routine of...

....
....

because ....

....

....

....

Today the person I give
thanks and gratitude for is...

....
....

because ....

....

....

....

My World

One thing that happened
in the world today for which
I am grateful is...

....

....

this is because ....

....

....

....

MEDITATION ON HAPPINESS

The most positive highlight
of my day was...

....

....

because ....

....

....

....

I appreciated nature's
powerful energy by...

....

....

....

....

....

HAPPY THOUGHTS

My positive affirmation of
gratitude before I sleep is...

....

....

....

....

....

....

My
small but
fulfilling accomplishment
today was...

....

....

....

....

....

Creative Visualization

Tomorrow I am most
looking forward to...

....

....

....

....

....

....

Evening Gratitude

Today I enjoyed
the daily routine of...

....
....

because ....

....

....

....

Today the person I give
thanks and gratitude for is...

....

....

because ....

....

....

....

My World

One thing that happened
in the world today for which
I am grateful is...

....

....

this is because ....

....

....

....

MEDITATION ON HAPPINESS

The most positive highlight
of my day was...

....

....

because ....

....

....

....

I appreciated nature's powerful energy by...

....

....

....

....

....

HAPPY THOUGHTS
My positive affirmation of gratitude before I sleep is...

....

....

....

....

....

....

My small but fulfilling accomplishment today was...

....

....

....

....

....

Creative Visualization
Tomorrow I am most looking forward to...

....

....

....

....

....

....

Evening Gratitude

Today I enjoyed
the daily routine of...

....

....

because ....

....

....

....

....

Today the person I give
thanks and gratitude for is...

....

....

because ....

....

....

....

....

My World

One thing that happened
in the world today for which
I am grateful is...

....

....

this is because ....

....

....

....

MEDITATION
ON HAPPINESS

The most positive highlight
of my day was...

....

....

because ....

....

....

....

I appreciated nature's
powerful energy by...

....

....

....

....

HAPPY THOUGHTS

My positive affirmation of
gratitude before I sleep is...

....

....

....

....

....

....

My
small but
fulfilling accomplishment
today was...

....

....

....

....

....

Creative Visualization

Tomorrow I am most
looking forward to...

....

....

....

....

....

....

Evening Gratitude

Today I enjoyed
the daily routine of...

....
....

because ....

....
....
....

Today the person I give
thanks and gratitude for is...

....

because ....

....
....
....

My World
One thing that happened
in the world today for which
I am grateful is...

....
....

this is because ....

....
....
....

MEDITATION
ON HAPPINESS
The most positive highlight
of my day was...

....
....

because ....

....
....
....

I appreciated nature's
powerful energy by...

....

....

....

....

....

HAPPY THOUGHTS
My positive affirmation of
gratitude before I sleep is...

....

....

....

....

....

My
small but
fulfilling accomplishment
today was...

....

....

....

....

....

Creative Visualization
Tomorrow I am most
looking forward to...

....

....

....

....

....

....

Evening Gratitude

Today I enjoyed
the daily routine of...

....

....

because ....

....

....

....

Today the person I give
thanks and gratitude for is...

....

....

because ....

....

....

....

My World
One thing that happened
in the world today for which
I am grateful is...

....

....

this is because ....

....

....

....

MEDITATION
ON HAPPINESS
The most positive highlight
of my day was...

....

....

because ....

....

....

....

I appreciated nature's
powerful energy by...

....

....

....

....

HAPPY THOUGHTS

My positive affirmation of
gratitude before I sleep is...

....

....

....

....

....

....

My
small but
fulfilling accomplishment
today was...

....

....

....

....

....

Creative Visualization

Tomorrow I am most
looking forward to...

....

....

....

....

....

....

Evening Gratitude

Today I enjoyed
the daily routine of...

....

....

because ....

....

....

....

Today the person I give
thanks and gratitude for is...

....

....

because ....

....

....

....

My World

One thing that happened
in the world today for which
I am grateful is...

....

....

this is because ....

....

....

....

MEDITATION ON HAPPINESS

The most positive highlight
of my day was...

....

....

because ....

....

....

....

I appreciated nature's powerful energy by...

....
....
....
....

HAPPY THOUGHTS

My positive affirmation of gratitude before I sleep is...

....
....
....
....
....
....

My small but fulfilling accomplishment today was...

....
....
....
....
....

Creative Visualization

Tomorrow I am most looking forward to...

....
....
....
....
....
....